No Longer Not Allowed

Amy Gingrich

NO LONGER NOT ALLOWED

iUniverse books may be ordered through booksellers or by contacting:

iUniverse
1663 Liberty Drive
Bloomington, IN 47403
www.iuniverse.com
1-800-Authors (1-800-288-4677)

Because of the dynamic nature of the Internet, any web addresses or links contained in this book may have changed since publication and may no longer be valid. The views expressed in this work are solely those of the author and do not necessarily reflect the views of the publisher, and the publisher hereby disclaims any responsibility for them.

Any people depicted in stock imagery provided by Thinkstock are models, and such images are being used for illustrative purposes only.
Certain stock imagery © Thinkstock.

ISBN: 978-1-4917-9171-4 (sc)
ISBN: 978-1-4917-9172-1 (e)

Library of Congress Control Number: 2016905451

Print information available on the last page.

iUniverse rev. date: 04/11/2016

Chapter 1

MSUD Explanation

Life with MSUD (maple syrup urine disease) is no picnic. First of all, the name of the disease itself is embarrassing. I mean, what sixteen- or seventeen-year-old girl wants to explain to her boyfriend about her disease? Really, having to say urine to a boy is humiliating. Plus there is the smell of maple syrup. Every girl likes to smell sweet to a boy, but with MSUD, to smell sickeningly sweet means something is wrong. MSUD is a metabolic disorder classified by the burned maple syrup smell in one's urine, ear wax, and body sweat. The smell gets stronger as the levels of protein in the blood get higher. Running high levels of protein can cause irreversible damage to a patient. The patient with MSUD cannot process three essential amino acids in protein—isoleucine, leucine, and valine. In order to keep the patient from suffering severe brain or physical damage, he or she must be diagnosed within four to seven days of birth. If diagnosed late, as many of my friends were, the patient can suffer from brain damage, seizures, blood toxicity, cerebral edema (brain swelling), and even death.

MSUD is a recessive disorder inherited from both parents. The chances of getting MSUD is one in four when both parents carry the gene. Imagine the genetic square box called the Punnett square. MSUD is has a big *T* and a little *t* on the top of box and on the left side of the box. If you put the *T*s together, you would have a box with two big *T*s, two boxes with a big *T* and a little *t* in each, and a final box with two little *t*s in it. My sister and I are the extremes of that box. She got the big *T*s (not a genetic carrier), and I got both small *t*s (have the genetic disease).

Besides the sweet smell of maple syrup in my urine, a couple of ways my mom could tell I had high levels was the intense lethargy I suffered from. She used to tell me that if I didn't even want to read my book or do anything I liked to do, she knew something was up. Another way to tell was with a "drunken" walk called ataxia. Ataxia happens when the leucine count in the blood is too high. It is known as the drunken walk because someone with ataxia walks slumped to the side, stumbling into doors, walls, and generally anything that gets in his or her way. It's a common condition—not fatal but not what the doctors want to see. MSUD is a fairly new disease, with the first case being diagnosed in 1959.

No one knows how many children died prior to 1959 due to being undiagnosed. Even after 1959, children would still die early because no one really knew how to treat MSUD. Doctors kind of learned on the fly what children could or couldn't tolerate. MSUD is treated by a strict diet and carefully monitoring symptoms of illness and food intake. MSUD is a disease in which the person cannot process protein normally. Because people with MSUD cannot hold protein in their muscles like "normal" people can, the energy level of someone with MSUD can be short lived. In other words, running, swimming, exercising, biking, and sometimes even skating can be really hard to do for long periods of time. For me, little things like jumping rope, biking, roller-skating, swimming, and even exercising for more than a half hour could prove dangerous to me. I get dizzy and short of breath, my heart pounds like crazy, and I feel weak. I hated knowing that I couldn't do the things I wanted to without having to rest. In school, gym class was a trying activity for me. I couldn't keep up with the other kids, resulting in my feeling nauseous and lightheaded and sometimes even vomiting.

My teacher didn't always believe I wasn't well enough to do the activity. I remember one time in middle school, we were told to run the mile. I knew I couldn't run it, so I told Dr. Holmes Morton (my MSUD specialist), and he told me that to run the mile could be dangerous for me. He wrote a note to my gym teacher excusing me from the mile, but she didn't believe me. She told me that the only reason I had a note was because I was too lazy to run the mile. She made me run the mile in spite of his note! Because of that, I ended up sick. I didn't run the mile; I jogged and walked it. I couldn't breathe by the time I was done. I was really upset by the whole thing, considering that I ruined my knee from that incident, and many people think I should have gone to the principal. I figured that if the teacher didn't believe me, why would the principal? The teacher never mentioned the incident after that, and I suffered from a badly strained knee cartilage muscle that healed incorrectly.

Once in middle school, a friend pulled a very dangerous stunt on me. I had gotten up to throw my trash away, and he thought it'd be funny to put his roll into my thermos of the special formula I had to drink. When I returned, I found the formula was undrinkable. My mother was very mad at him for that. It may not have seemed dangerous to anyone, but it could have caused my levels to go out of control. You see, with MSUD, getting sick is very tricky. A simple cold can push my levels higher than normal, and the fight to bring them back down again becomes a power struggle. If I did get sick but couldn't keep down the formula or anything else, then I would end up in the hospital with an IV in my arm.

I was glad to leave the middle school scene for high school. I joined marching band at the end of my freshman year and found I could actually tolerate the strenuous schedule and marching with a six-foot flagpole. I loved the crowds and the sounds, sights, smells, and tastes of marching band. The instructors I had in marching band were very patient with me. They understood that with my disease, I couldn't handle marching the entire show, so I marched the beginning, the entire middle section, and the very end. The rest of the show, I was considered a runner, someone who helps collect discarded flags and props when the color guard members are done with them.

In marching band I started to build an endurance that I otherwise would not have gotten, but in my senior year, there was a complete staff turnover. The new staff forced me to march the entire show, as I was one of the four senior guard members. I had a lot of trouble with my knee swelling during those long, hot band-camp days. I had to wrap my knee every day at band camp just to march correctly. An MRI showed that my right knee (injured in middle school) had severe arthritis and calcium deposits, making my right knee considerably larger than my left knee. To this day, I still have problems with that knee, especially if I've worked it too hard.

Throughout high school, I was placed in mainstream classes and made decent grades. I had trouble in a lot of classes dealing with math and science. I learn best hands on, and my fine motor skills weren't up to par with my classmates. I was glad I didn't have to be in special education classes, but I was aware that my courses were harder than normal for me. I took Algebra 1 in two years and still barely passed with a C in both classes. In my junior year, I took general chemistry (I was told I would need chemistry to attend the nursing vo-tech program) and barely passed with a D, and that was with a tutor who luckily was very patient with me. I loved my hands-on classes, like ceramics and textiles. These classes allowed my creativity to show through big-time!

Like any MSUD patient, I've had more than my fair share of hospitalizations. Since I was born, I've been hospitalized about a dozen times for various illnesses. Of the common illnesses a child can get, dehydration and pneumonia are the two killers for MSUD patients. Both can wreak serious havoc on the body's system with levels and can cause serious damage to the brain. In school, kids would call me names like "baby," "freak," and "weirdo." It hurt but not as much as that prank I told you about earlier. As for the friend who played that prank, he was laughing the whole time while I was trying to figure out what to do with the formula. He had no explanation for why he did it, except that he thought it would be funny. He didn't realize how dangerous it could have been for me.

All my life, I was told there is no cure for MSUD, so I believed I would be strange forever. I knew I ate differently, smelled weird, and was different from my peers. When I was twelve, Dr. Morton, my specialist, told me that a liver transplant was done on an eight-year-old with MSUD because she would have died without it. She had vitamin A toxicity, and her life was threatened because of the liver being killed. Dr. Morton had told my parents before the girl's transplant that he suspected a majority of MSUD was based in the liver since that's where the enzymes were that couldn't break down the proteins. The transplant for this girl was successful, and just like Dr. Morton thought, her symptoms of MSUD went away. Genetically she still had the disease, but she was no longer restricted to a special diet. Dr. Morton told me that at that point, insurance companies weren't considering the transplants as medically necessary, so that wasn't an option. That was okay with me. I had learned to live with my genetic prison. That's how I saw my disease—as a prison. I was feeling trapped by having to watch everything I ate, and it had a ball and chain effect. With MSUD, a person's body will slowly start to wear out from the lack of protein in the diet. The organs will start to shut down or cease to function gradually as the child gets older. The body will begin to break itself down, and the levels will become increasingly hard to control.

Chapter 2

The Road to Transplant

About nine years after the first transplant for MSUD, doctors started looking at transplants a little more closely. I didn't think about transplant too much since I was healthy. A lot of my friends were dealing with health crises. They weren't healthy anymore. Some of them were having to be hospitalized more and more, and it was starting to take a toll on their bodies. It took Drs. Morton and Kevin Strauss writing medically necessary letters to the insurance companies for them to approve the transplants. Before Dr. Morton started writing the letters, insurance companies fought to not approve the transplants. In 2004, the first MSUD transplant since 1995 was done for a four-year-old boy from Fairfax, Virginia.

The transplant was done at Children's Hospital of Pittsburgh under the care of Dr. George Mazariegos. I was a bit leery about the whole thing because it seemed too good to be true. My mom and dad talked a lot with Dr. Morton, and he highly recommended it since I was getting too old to be considered pediatric anymore. There were no doctors that treated adults living with MSUD. Drs. Morton and Strauss were pediatricians, but they treated about twenty-eight adult MSUD patients. My parents and I decided to at least go out to Pittsburgh for a consultation. It couldn't hurt, and if I still wasn't sure, I could always say no. I had just started working full-time at Welsh Mountain Medical and Dental Center, and I even had my own insurance—Health America.

My mother was submitting my medical bills for my formula, and the insurance company paid $1,500 a month for it. They would pay my bills, but it was costly for them. When we finally decided to go for a consultation, Dr. Morton wrote to the insurance company, which agreed to pay for the consultation plus travel expenses.

Squrriel Hill Tunnel at 7am

In July 2005, my parents and I headed out to Pittsburgh for a three-day consultation. We met with a variety of people—transplant doctors, radiologists, anesthesiologists, and a few other people—who completely bombarded us with information. The information we were given was terrifying, as the doctors were giving us worst-case scenarios and horrifying side effects. My parents could see that I was being drained of energy, so they asked the doctors to give us some time to think, pray, and discuss this before giving our answer.

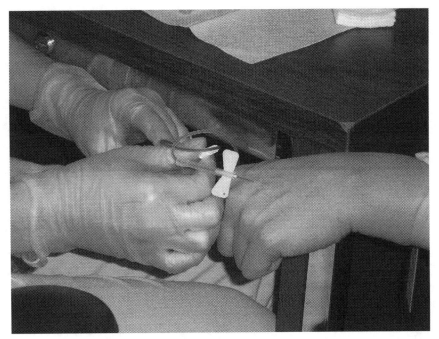

lab draw

As part of the testing, the lab techs had to draw thirteen tubes of blood from me the first day (fasting) and an additional tube the next day. The doctors told us to take our time; there was no rush. It was not a decision to be taken lightly. It was to be life changing for me and for my family.

We came home and used our time to argue and discuss the ups and downs, pros and cons of transplant. Suddenly, I could be normal, but I wasn't sure it was worth the risk. MSUD was my identity, and I couldn't just shed it like a snake. I often use the comparison of Linus from the *Peanuts* cartoon. Linus has a security blanket with him at all times, but if you take that blanket away from him, he no longer feels secure. He becomes light-headed, dizzy, and short of breath, and in general he's out of control until you give it back. That's how I felt with MSUD—it was my security blanket. I knew all about my disease and what I could and couldn't have to eat. However, my mother wisely realized before I did that if I wanted to move out of her house and live on my own, I was going to have to do this. If I were to get sick, would I know that my levels were up or that I needed help? Would I compromise my life or someone else's life? Finally, I agreed to be listed, and in November 2005, I was listed with a very low score. I thought, *Well, I'm not going to be called any time soon, so I'll just keep working.* My coworkers could see the deterioration of my mental capacity. They described me later as being foggy and unfocused, which is an apt description of what was happening to me. MSUD clouds the mind and makes it difficult to make rational decisions.

Many MSUD patients get older, but their minds (reasoning and decision making) are those of a child. The disease ages the body but not the mind, at least not right away. When the mind catches up, suddenly the "child" is old. While the body gets older, the face tends to stay young. A patient could be thirty-five years old and still look like he or she is only sixteen. Case in point, at age nineteen, people would ask me if I was in middle school yet. At age eighteen, my mother, sister, and I went out to eat at a buffet restaurant. It was a place had a discount for children under twelve years old. The guy behind the cash register asked if there was anyone in our party under twelve, and he looked right at me! I knew I was short and looked much younger, but good grief! I told him I was eighteen, and he only looked away without saying anything.

One thing I noticed at work was I went from happy and content to being explosive and angry. I couldn't take jokes (I thought they were a slam against me), I couldn't figure out how to make my mouth say what my brain was thinking, and I was easily distracted, and it showed in my work. Only by the grace of my boss did I last six years and eleven months at my job. But in the meantime, I wasn't me anymore. I couldn't understand how to live with this genetic curse anymore. I wanted to be free. I found that my concentration at work was next to impossible, and no one wanted to pull pranks on me because I would fly off the handle at the dumbest things.

Chapter 3

The Call for a Transplant

On January 10, 2006, I was sound asleep, and my cell phone rang at about eleven thirty at night. I had only been listed for about two months and never dreamed I would be called so quickly. I answered the phone to find out it was the transplant team saying they had a liver for me. You can imagine I woke up pretty quickly. I woke up my parents and told them what was happening. My mom spoke with the team a bit, asking them questions about the liver.

I was completely freaking out, saying, "I'm not ready! I don't have anything packed, nothing squared away at work, and I'm just not ready!"

My mom could see that I wasn't ready, and she asked, "If we pass on this liver, will it affect our chances of getting called again?"

They told her it wouldn't, so we passed on the liver. I tell you, that was my wakeup call! I realized the next time might be my last chance, and I had to be on top of things if I was going to do this. Later on that next day, my mom called our coordinator to see if I was the main call or the alternate. With transplants, doctors will call a main person (the patient receiving the organ) and one alternate patient. That way, if the main person can't make it for some reason, they have someone else who can take the organ.

Pittsburgh told us that night I would have driven all the way out there only to drive home the next day. In other words, I was the backup patient. I also found out a lot later that a friend of mine with MSUD was the next person they called after me to be the alternate. I went to work the day after that call and told my boss that we had a mild scare the night before when Pittsburgh called me with a liver. She helped me get prepared for the next call, giving me all the necessary paperwork for disability insurance and other papers. My mom and I took time to pack a duffel bag for me with loose clothing for the hospital.

That way I would have clothing to wear in the apartment when I came out of the hospital. Then came the mental preparation for the fact that the doctors were going to slice open my body and replace an organ. That wasn't so bad. I wasn't crazy about them cutting me open, but I figured it was better than dying young.

About two weeks after that initial phone call, a call came in at about nine at night on our house phone. It was January 22, 2006, and my family was all at home. My sister was working on homework, I was getting ready for bed, and my parents had just gotten home from a walk. When the phone rang, my dad was the closest one to it.

He jokingly said, "It's Pittsburgh!" and when he said hello, they asked for me.

"Hello?"

"Is this Amy?"

"Yes it is."

"This is Pittsburgh. We've got a liver for you!"

"Oh my word! It is them! It is!" This conversation happened in a span of about a minute.

My dad was as shocked as I was while my mom and sister ran in to listen to the call. The first thing I asked was,

"Is it for me? Am I the main person?" They said yes and asked how quickly could I get there? I told them we could be out there within the six-hour window they gave us, and they said,

"That's fine. We'll be waiting for you."

After I hung up the phone, my sister fell back against the wall in shock. "This is for real!" she kept saying.

It couldn't have come at a better time. She was doing her graduation project on the before and after effects of MSUD and transplant. Four people had never packed an SUV so quickly. Within a half hour after that call, we were on our way to Pittsburgh. In the car, Mom, Audrey, and I started making phone calls to various people to let them know I was headed for the transplant.

When I called my boss, she screamed so loud she nearly broke my eardrums! She was so happy for me, but during the call, we went through a dead zone, and I lost her. When I could finally call her back, she was busy calling all my coworkers. My mom called our pastor to let him know to start the phone tree so people could know what was going on.

The message left on our machine about the transplant was the following: "I apologize for the lateness of this call, but we've had an urgent prayer request that we were asked to pass on to you. We just received word that the Zimmerman family is on their way to Pittsburgh and that Amy will receive her transplant tonight. They would really like our prayers for safety as they travel throughout the night and possibly go through with this transplant."

Since the call came in so late at night, it was amazing that people actually got their families together to pray for us. Mom also called the highway patrol that night to let them know we were going for a transplant. They offered to escort us, but Mom said we'd be fine. We were kind of concerned because it was wintertime, and it was rainy. The rain on the road made for a slick trip, but we arrived safely in Pittsburgh at about one o'clock in the morning on January 23. I think that night I was the only one who slept on the way out.

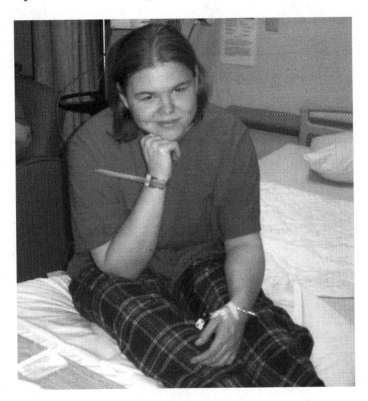

When we got to Children's Hospital of Pittsburgh at about one o'clock, the place was dead. Because it was so late, we had to register at the emergency room entrance and go up to seventh floor, which is the transplant floor. The nurses there were very kind to my family and me as they did test after test to determine whether I was good to go. The tests took a long time, and my parents and I slept in the room we were waiting in as my sister explored the floor with her video camera.

I found out later from my mom that the transplant doctors called Dr. Morton because they were concerned about my levels being a little elevated. (I'd had a latte with real milk in it the night before.) From what my mom told me, they weren't sure they should do the surgery with my levels being the way they were, but Dr. Morton told them, "Transplant her quick, and the levels will straighten out."

At about five in the morning, the tests complete, the nurses woke me up to give me the first dose of Prograf, the antirejection medication. After they had everything finalized, they wheeled me down to the prep room, where they put anesthesia into my IV line. I don't remember what I said, but it must have been funny because the last thing I remember hearing was laughter. In no time at all, I was out cold, and that's the last thing I remember for a long time. My parents told me later that the surgery took nine hours, but it went well.

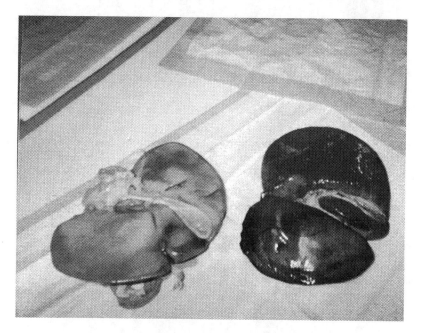

Dr. Sindhi came out to tell my parents that my new liver wasn't getting enough blood through my arteries, so they used the carotid artery of my donor to reconstruct the main artery to my liver. With MSUD patients, there are two main differences with the liver: (1) The liver has three small arteries feeding it, rather than one main artery, and (2) the liver, instead of being a deep red color, is a yellowish color. All in all, the surgery went as expected, and I was moved to PICU (Pediatric Intensive Care Unit). My parents were allowed to come see me whenever they wanted to but only for about ten minutes at a time.

I'm not sure how long it was till I came out of the anesthesia, but it was a long time. My parents told me that they weren't prepared for the number of machines and monitors that were attached to me.

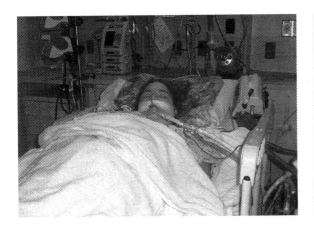 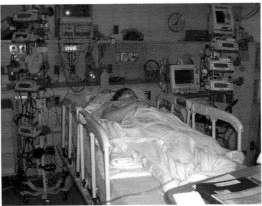

I had a ventilator and a nasogastric tube (NG tube), along with a heart monitor (attached to my finger), blood pressure gauge, solution (not exactly sure what) drip bag into my IV, and more bells and whistles than I even know.

My father later said on the video my sister made, "I wasn't prepared to see her like that, and it really hurt me to know that I pushed for this. Suddenly, here's my daughter and I feel helpless, like there is nothing I can do for her now. Now I'm wondering if I made the right choice in pushing for this."

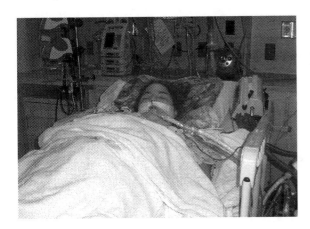 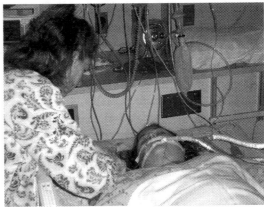

Audrey also said on the video, "It didn't look the Amy I knew. I mean, I had just seen her healthy and breathing, and now it looked like she was in a terrible car accident."

It was really hard on all of my family to see me after transplant because I couldn't acknowledge that they were with me. When I finally came to a little bit, the first person I remember seeing was Audrey. She couldn't sleep, so she came down to the ICU to see me.

She whispered to me, "Amy, you don't have MSUD anymore."

I surprised her by slowly lifting up my hand with the IV sticking out of it and giving her a thumbs up. I'm not really sure what caused me to wake up, whether it was simply the anesthesia wearing off or the nurse adjusting my line or the cries of the infants that were in the ICU with me.

Chapter 4

The Road to Recovery

The next time I became conscious, Mom and Audrey were with me. Because I had the breathing tube in, I couldn't talk. I couldn't hold a pencil steady, I couldn't really see straight (everything just kind of swam to the left), and my eyelids felt like they were loaded with bricks, but I wanted to communicate.

Audrey and I both know sign language, so I decided to use it. Looking back, I realize it was the only form of communication I didn't have to stay awake for; I could form words with my hands and still keep my eyes closed. I started to sign something, and my mom asked Audrey to interpret for me. I didn't have enough strength in my hands to form whole letters, but after a few guesses, they finally understood. The first thing I signed to them was t-e-d-d-y. I had brought my teddy bear along, but somehow he got left in the car. Mom went to get him for me, and then they began to ask me easy questions. Because I was still kind of dopey, it was a chore for me to try to focus on the conversations around me, so I often closed my eyes to just listen. My cousin accused me of falling asleep on her when she came to see me in the ICU, but I assured her I knew she was there.

What most of the people who came to see me during that time didn't realize was that every time I opened my eyes, everything I saw was blurry and unfocused. It was a lot easier to just open briefly to see who was with me and then close them again to just listen. I couldn't really talk with anyone, so what was the point? The doctors were really concerned about me in the ICU because I had blood pressures of 160/112, which is too high for anyone, let alone a twenty-one-year-old girl. I started having hiccups almost twenty-four hours after the initial surgery, so the doctors did an ultrasound and found blood pooling behind my new liver. These hiccups were not like regular hiccups. For one thing, I had them with tubes in my mouth, so there was no way of stopping them myself. My sister told me that she thought something was wrong with me because my body started to jerk like I was seizing.

They had to take me back into surgery to drain that blood pool, which meant they had to remove my fifty-eight staples and then put them back into my abdomen. That was not fun for me. After about four and half days, the doctors decided I was better enough to be moved to the seventh floor—the transplant floor. This was after I had a bad reaction to one of my medications. I remember being asleep and waking up to a weight in my chest. It felt like I couldn't quite catch my breath. I was drawing air in, but I couldn't release any of it! My legs started to violently shake, and I remember the feeling of sheer panic that I couldn't breathe. When my legs started to shake, my mom was with me, and she got a nurse. She said it was a normal reaction to one of the medications and gave me another one to calm me down. It took a while for me to finally really relax and breathe. I just remember being so scared that I couldn't breathe, and I couldn't make anyone realize that I couldn't breathe.

When I was finally moved to 7N, which is what they called the transplant floor, I wasn't a happy camper. I was sick, in pain, and wishing I could just go back to the way I knew. Of course, that wasn't ever going to happen, so I had to deal with it. I had trouble eating foods because I wasn't used to the absolute freedom I now had. Most people have no problem eating whatever, but everything I ate prior to transplant tasted basically the same. There were so many medications to remember to take, and a couple of them tasted horrible! Too many unusual choices of food made it difficult for me to get used to eating normally. The amount of protein I was allowed to consume before transplant on a good day was equal of that of an eight-ounce glass of milk. I know I frustrated everyone when I would only eat foods I was familiar with, like potatoes and rice.

I was completely frustrated with myself because I knew in my heart I could eat anything I wanted to, but it had been ingrained into me since I was born that if I ate that, I would get very, very sick. I couldn't make myself eat what I wasn't familiar with, and no one except someone who has been there knows exactly what I mean. I couldn't read anything because so much of my medication made everything swim to the left. In other words, it was like reading underwater.

I love to read, even when I have no time to read, so this was a major problem for me. To ask my mother, nurse, sister, or anyone else to read to me was hard. For one thing, I was in the middle of a book that had words that were hard to pronounce, and it wasn't fun for me. I was assigned a physical therapist who was supposed to help me with some exercises and walking around the floor. Because I was sitting in bed all day, I wasn't gaining any muscle strength, so the PT nurse would help me with walking and exercising to gain strength. However, I was *anything* but a model patient. I gave him, my nurses, my doctors, my mother, and just about anyone who came to see me a very hard time. I am ashamed to say that I fought my therapist in every way. I was rude to the nurses, fought the doctors, and generally felt sorry for myself. I'm not at all proud of how I acted and have since apologized to as many people as I could, and everyone told me that they forgave me. I believe now that being sick and in pain caused a major attitude breakdown, but that's no excuse. The medications, the stress of surgery, and not feeling good made me a horrible person to be around

Despite measures to keep me from catching an illness, I managed to catch a cold in the ICU. The doctors told me that due to my immunosuppression, it would take longer to recover from it than normal. I had to have blood work drawn two times a day in the hospital, but they couldn't use my IV lines. Since they were drawing blood out of me so often, my veins kept collapsing on them. At the end of my fifteen-day torturous (that's what it felt like to me) stay, my arms from my elbows to fingertips were black, blue, and purple from being stuck so much. They probably could have used the central line in my neck (and they did a few times), but that was arterial blood and very different from the venous blood they needed.

While I was in Pittsburgh Children's Hospital the first time was over the Super Bowl of 2006, in which my beloved Steelers played against the Seattle Seahawks and won 21 to 7! The entire city went topsy-turvy and nuts about the Steelers being in the Super Bowl. The nurses and doctors got into the madness by wearing jerseys and Steelers colors. The floor was totally decorated, and the playroom activities were all Steelers stuff. My mother and I made some door decorations. The night of the game, every TV on the floor was on. The nurses made their rounds and managed to watch the game with us that night. Someone generously donated a stack of Terrible Towels to the hospital, so Jacki, our playroom director, passed them out.

I now own three Terrible Towels because my aunt and uncle, who live in Pittsburgh, brought me two towels and a Steelers popcorn container that is also a piggybank. Back to the Super Bowl. For every touchdown that the Steelers got, the entire floor would erupt into cheers. My mom and dad were with me for almost the whole game. You see, the shuttle bus from the hotel only ran until nine thirty, so my parents couldn't stay beyond halftime. It was okay, though, because I knew they would come back. They always did, and they always loved me no matter what. Later, when the Super Bowl was over, we started hearing sirens, and all kinds of things were happening. I caught the night nurse, who was doing my vitals, and asked her what in the world was going on. She told me that there was a riot in downtown Oakland, where the hospital was, and some of the rioters had overturned three cars! My parents told me the next day that a police motorcade had driven past their hotel with the sirens wailing.

When I finally got to leave the hospital, I still wasn't well. I had tried a little bit of new food, but I didn't like the texture of it. On the videotape my sister made, my mother was videotaping me soon after getting into my new room. Dad was helping me eat a meal I had ordered. It was Salisbury steak, mashed potatoes, and peas.

He said, "You eat that all up. It will give you strength. That's good food," while feeding me a few bites of the steak. After that phrase, he quickly put down the fork and said, "You can feed yourself! Your arms aren't broke!"

My mom can be heard laughing in the background. I looked at my mom and said to the camera, "It's not bad. Not my favorite, but not bad."

To me, everything new tasted weird. I wasn't used to it at all. At the hotel, which we rented for a month at a time (it was for hospital patients and their families), I had two MSUD friends who also had transplants at the same time. When I felt well enough, I would join them at the hotel pool and we would chill. Some days were a lot rougher than others. I argued about eating with my mother. No, I was not an anorexic, but I couldn't force myself to eat much. I didn't want to eat since nothing tasted good to me, and my parents didn't understand that. I realize now that it was good for my mother to have the other two moms of the MSUD friends because she could tell them about her frustrations with me and get some advice or a shoulder to cry on if she needed it.

About two weeks and four clinic visits after I got out of the hospital, the doctors decided to change my antirejection medication since the lab work was showing decreased kidney function. They told me that my kidneys had taken a hard hit from surgery, and the immunosuppression drug dosage wasn't helping anything.

Their exact wording was, "Your kidney function is a bit sluggish, and we are concerned about it. If we don't correct it soon, in time you will need a kidney transplant too."

That scared me since I was still having a lot of pain from the liver transplant. The doctors put me back in the hospital to change the meds. I was now taking a more organ-friendly drug called Rapamune. Although it didn't offer the same protection as Prograf, they wanted to make sure that my kidneys were not as sluggish as they seemed. I didn't like the thought of taking any new medications because the "old" medications were hard enough to get used to taking each day. They did blood work every day, but it takes thirty-six hours to get the antirejection levels back.

During this stay, my two friends at the hotel were discharged to go home, so they both came to see me one last time. The girl, whom I'll call Bri, had no troubles with her transplant whatsoever, and I had never hated anyone so much. I didn't really hate her—she's one of my closest friends—but I was so jealous that she wasn't sick or anything. She didn't even have trouble eating, and she was able to tolerate much less protein than me prior to transplant! The boy, whom I'll simply call E, had a few issues that I didn't have, such as pancreatitis or an inflammation of the pancreas, which made him really sick. Anyway, when they left, I was still in the hospital and still not better. Four days after they put me in the hospital, they allowed me to go back to the hotel.

Chapter 5

Slow Recovery

After that second discharge to the hotel, I was on so much medication that all I did was wait to take meds and blood pressures all day. My sickness got worse a couple of days later. I started coughing more, and it was a harsh, hacking cough accompanied by vomiting at least four times a day, constant nausea, low-grade fever, and lots of crying and yelling. I was angry with everyone around me because no one, including my parents, believed it was anything more than a bad cold, and the doctors had convinced my parents it was all in my head. My parents kept asking what was wrong with me, but the doctors said, "It's just a cold, and it will go away in time." Time and time again, my parents were quick to remind me that I wasn't keeping my end of the bargain.

I had made a bargain with Dr. Sindhi that if he would let me off the nystatin swish and swallow mouthwash for thrush early, I would eat two bites of something new twice a day. I'm sorry to say I wasn't really good at that, but come on, give me some credit—I couldn't keep anything down long enough to do me any good, and besides, nothing tasted good to me. I said on my sister's video that when you don't feel good, nothing tastes good.

Walking, which I still had to do, would trigger a coughing fit, vomiting, or both. I didn't want to go anywhere or do anything because I didn't want to get sick. Basically, I could count on getting up in the morning and vomiting right away, along with any other time during the day. I sucked down more cough drops than I can count. My mother had gotten a Vicks vaporizer plug in for the wall, and I even tried my inhaler, but nothing stopped the coughing.

It was during these weeks that I questioned a lot of things, including my faith. I wondered if all this hassle was really worth it. My pastor and his wife were very patient with me as I questioned why God would allow me to go through so much pain. Clinic visit after clinic visit was a disappointment to me as the doctors continued to tell me there was nothing wrong with me. I wonder if they even tried to get my parents to take me to a shrink. I think if I had used the following analogy with them if I may have gotten help sooner. Take a stress reliever ball in your hand, and squeeze it really hard. Release it quickly, and feel it suction back into place. That's what was happening to my right lung every time I coughed. I would lay on the daybed in the hotel room and feel the bubbling with every breath.

I was losing weight rapidly since I had no appetite and couldn't keep anything down. I was to a point where I just wanted to grab that doctor by his jacket and shake him to death, yelling, "Why won't you listen to me? I'm the patient, not my mother! She doesn't feel sick all the time, cough her lungs up with every breath, or hear and feel the bubbling in her chest! It's not her, it's me! I'm the patient! I know something is wrong!"

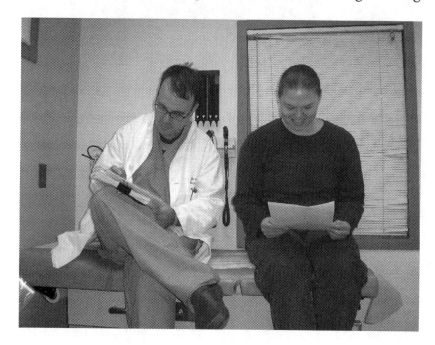

Finally, Dr. Soltys agreed to listen to my lungs again. They had been doing this for weeks, and I told him this time it had to be a different test. He had me to breathe in and out really fast while he listened. He told my mother that he thought he heard something, but he couldn't be sure so we'd get a chest x-ray to check it out. It turned out, I was right about something being really wrong. I had a condition called a pulmonary effusion or fluid in the space around my lung, not in it.

This effusion made it difficult for the doctors to hear right away, which is why they didn't know I had it. They decided to admit me into the hospital to drain the fluid. My mom and I went to registration, where I laid down to try to breathe without coughing. Mom and I both thought I would only be in the hospital for a few days. They let me go up to the room finally, and then came the IVs and preparations for taking me down to the operating room. I remember thinking, *How is it going to feel? Are they going to give me something to numb the pain? Is it going to hurt?* They propped me up on something that felt like a board. I was told to lean forward and rest my head on my arms. They must have put anesthesia in my IV line, because when I woke up, I was back in my room, laying on something sticking out of my back.

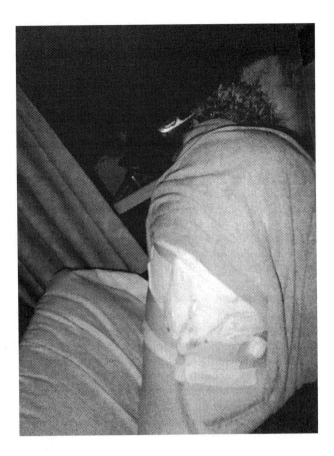

They had placed a chest tube in my back around my shoulder blade area. It hurt to breathe and cough. That first day or two, the doctors figured they drained about one liter of fluid from around my right lung. Now I know why when you are in the hospital after a procedure, they tell you to cough every few hours (and not a little puny cough either but a deep cough)—to keep from getting this condition. While I was finally able to breathe a little bit, I still didn't seem to be getting any better. They ran blood work every day till my hands were black and blue, but no rejection showed up, so they never suspected it.

During this fifteen-day hospital stay, I had four roommates. Two of them were only twenty-four-hour stays, so I didn't have time to get to know them, but the other two girls were my friends. Both of them were eight years old and just the sweetest girls that a person could know. One of the girls, Melissa, was a shy little girl suffering from wacky Coumadin levels. Her parents and grandparents came to see not only her but me as well. Mel and I became close despite the age difference (thirteen years). Both of us stayed in bed, her because she was too weak to get out of bed more than necessary and me because of the chest tube (although I was told to take three walks a day around the floor). Since neither of us could make it to the playroom, Jacki brought the playroom to us. Mel loved to color, and Jacki would bring her crayons, paints, paper, and one time even fake stained glass. Mel made me a stained glass butterfly keychain, and I still have it to this day. When she was allowed to go home a week after I got there, her dad came to get her.

He was so nice to my mom and me, and we had some really good conversations. He found out I was a Steelers fan, and during one of his visits, he brought me a Big Ben mug and a Steelers defense T-shirt, both of which I still have today. When Mel's grandparents came one time, they brought her a little stuffed pony that had her name velcroed to the butt. I was surprised when they came back a little later with one for me! I couldn't believe these people who didn't know me would bring a stuffed pony for me. Before Mel and her dad left the hospital, Mel picked out a blue balloon for me that said, "Get Well Soon" with some pretty yellow flowers on it. I miss her still and hope she is doing well.

I feel bad that I never got to get her any gifts even though she and her family gave me a lot of gifts. Every time they did her vital signs, I wanted to hug her tight because I knew how much it hurt her. She would cry and plead with the nurses not to hurt her anymore. It tugged my heart then, and it still does today.

My other roommate, whom I will not name, wore me out! Mel was quiet, but this little girl was like the energizer bunny! Despite being there for rejection of a stomach transplant when she was a baby, she just kept moving like crazy. I don't think I've ever seen an eight-year-old who was sick act as healthy as she did. I'll never forget what she said to me that first day when the nurses moved her into my room. She was as tall as my hip (I am only five-foot-four) and very skinny, but her eyes were shiny and she spoke clearly. She told me her name and asked who I was.

"My name is Amy," she said, looking at me. "I'm eight years old. How old are you?"

"How old do you think I am?"

She looked me up and down and said, "Twelve."

I looked at her and said, "Honey, I'm twenty-one."

She looked me up and down again and said, "You're short!"

I had to keep from laughing because I knew she was serious, but it was just too funny hearing it come from a girl half my height. All I knew was that she was alone in this hospital because her parents lived in the next state. The nurses felt I could keep an eye on her so much better than they could, what with them working and all. She would go on walks around the floor with me, but it wasn't a normal walk. I would walk and kind of slow and painfully, while she would bounce like her feet had springs in them. I wanted to call her Tigger sometimes. On the days I felt well enough, we would go to the playroom together. Jacki had her hands full with that child, so I became a helper in the playroom. I was the oldest mobile patient on the floor. (There was a girl there who was a year older than me, but she didn't come to the playroom because she was battling a lot of complications from a five-organ transplant two weeks before me.)

One day when the playroom was very full, Jacki said, "We are going to restock the rice table."

Have you ever tried to dye rice with eight children? It's mass chaos! I took it upon myself to use a glove to check the rice when each child was done dyeing it.

My girl was playing with the purple dye! You were only supposed to use a few drops, but she decided that wasn't enough for her. She wanted to douse the rice with purple dye! There was a young girl there suffering from jaundice, but that wasn't her only problem. She was deaf as well. I got to use my limited sign language and slow lip talk to let her know what we were doing and who we were. I think some of my best memories I have of the hospital were in that playroom. I made all kinds of friends there, and not one of them was older than me. In fact, most of them were under ten years old.

Every time a nurse did vital signs on me, I was still showing a fever, low grade, of course. That concerned the doctors, so they decided a biopsy on the liver would be best. I told them I wanted to be put under so I don't feel them sticking the long needle into my ribcage.

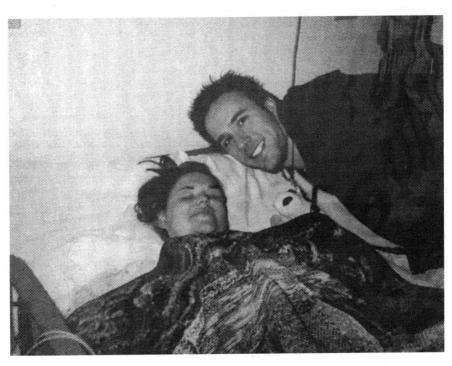

I learned later that my cousin, whom I thought hadn't come to see me, was there afterward, and apparently he was giving me a hard time. I don't remember anything about this visit, but I was told I was trying to hit his arm.

My pastor's wife came out during this stay to relieve my mother. My mom had been with me this whole time, and it was very stressful on her. She got to go home for a week and relax by catching up on things there. It was Lidia who was with me when they started giving me steroids for rejection. My mom and sister had been with me when Dr. M had said it was time to pull the first chest tube (yes, I said first). When they put it in, they had stitched it in place so it wouldn't fall out. When they took it out, they were tugging and cutting the stitches, and it hurt very badly.

When they did the biopsy, the results showed I was rejecting the new liver. Now, when I tell that to people, everyone always wonders if that meant I needed to get a new liver. No, that's not how it works. The only way that would happen was if I quit taking all medications and didn't take care of myself. When I asked them why they didn't know I was rejecting sooner, I was told that the particular way my rejection came up—getting really sick and pulmonary effusion—had only happened two other times.

It was Lidia who was with me when the doctors told me that the daily chest x-rays showed another pocket of fluid in my chest cavity. She explained to me what the doctors didn't explain very well. She told me they were going to put another chest tube in my lung. The doctor told me that they couldn't put me under again, so I had to drink a really chalky, gross, fake cherry-flavored liquid, which made me gag so bad, so I would be out of it enough to put my tube in.

When the doctors did a chest x-ray to make sure the second tube was in properly, they noticed something else was wrong. They tried to explain it to me, but Lidia broke it down in easier terms for me. The amount of fluid that was in my chest cavity (which they had already pulled out—over four liters altogether) had collapsed the lowest lobe of my right lung, the lung over the new liver. Your lungs are broken into lobes. The left lung has two lobes, and the right lung has three lobes. I was given a gizmo that measures how much lung capacity I had. I had to draw in a deep breath slowly, pulling the plastic bobbin inside to the top of the monitor. The higher the bobbin went, the more lung space I had.

In order to rebuild my lung space back, I had to do this exercise six times an hour, every ten minutes, even when I watching TV. This order came from the pulmonologists who were assigned to my case. Dr. M started me on the steroids with the first tube, and the steroids given to me were prednisone and celcept, first in an IV and later in oral meds. The steroids made my face get really puffy and fat. It hurt to smile, so during that time I quit smiling. Because of the steroids, my blood sugar was kicked sky high. I had to watch everything I ate again. I had to get stuck three times a day for blood sugar readings, be giving insulin every evening, and not eat anything for two hours before I took my blood sugar test. That was torture for me. You see, up to this point, I had to force myself to eat because I had no appetite and what little food I did eat didn't stay down. The prednisone really increased my appetite, and my mom and I went to buffet lines (when I was released from the hospital and hotel to go home) for lunch.

My aunt, who is a nurse, told my mom that like a little baby trying new foods, I needed to eat little bits of each food about ten times to acquire a taste for them. Buffet lines were the easiest way because then I could pick the amount of food I could eat. Once I learned how to stick myself with the little needles and insulin shots and learned about the medications and blood pressure readings, I was allowed to go back to the apartment. Before, when they were giving me the IV steroids, they wanted to put in a PICC line in my arm. I told them I wanted to be out for that, and they told me that is not something they do. It was no surprise to me that when they tried in my right arm, they nicked an artery. Next, they tried the left arm, but the vein was constricting—badly. I was lying on the table crying as they continued to try to push the wire up through the constricted vein. I was pleading with the doctor to please stop hurting me.

She told me, "If you don't stop crying, I'm going to stop."

I told her that's what I wanted her to do. Finally, they gave up and bandaged my arm. The doctors had to be careful doing blood pressures after that. Back at the hotel, my mom and I had a schedule of meds and multiple instructions to take blood pressures and temps. One really cool thing about the hotel was that they had breakfast all week and supper till Thursday, and each room had a schedule of what they would serve for the whole month (subject to changes, of course). Before my rejection, we were taking blood pressures due to the high readings in the ICU. We had been taking temps when I got sick to check for fevers, which I had the whole time.

During the rejection, I had lost a lot of weight, a total of thirty pounds in one month from vomiting and not eating. I ate more food on the prednisone, but most foods I wasn't familiar with had a metallic taste. I was on 80 mg of Prednisone a day and 1,000 mg of Celcept twice a day. I couldn't believe all the medicines I had to take—a whole little countertop full of meds! I started out with twelve meds a day, and gradually we were able to drop some of them. With the rejection, I hadn't been taking the nystatin mouthwash, so Mom was watching me closely for signs that I had thrush. Sure enough, I got thrush, albeit very lightly. Thanks to my mom, we caught it very early, and I felt no pain. Although

I had not been taking the nystatin, I had to take it again—four times a day for a month! I gagged so badly on it, and to this day, I can't eat Ice Breaker mints since I used them to cover the taste. With nystatin, you can't eat or drink anything for fifteen minutes after to let it coat your mouth and throat.

Chapter 6

Home Again

The nystatin was a sickeningly sweet swish and swallow mouthwash to treat or prevent thrush. I was allowed to suck on Ice Breaker mints, but they didn't always help. Toward the end, a Listerine strip was the only thing strong enough to cover the awful taste. I'm sure that if the doctors from Pittsburgh read this, I would get a lecture from them. Finally, after nine long weeks in Pittsburgh, I was allowed to go home for two whole weeks. My family was so happy that I could come home! Just a week or so before, I had commented to Mom that spring was coming without me, and I am a country girl. All that time, I had been living in Pittsburgh (either in the hospital or the hotel) ... for nine weeks! Nine very long weeks! Each day dragged by, but I was so sick I couldn't really do anything. Even so, just the possibility of going home to my house, my bed, and my cat was heaven.

You would understand if you have been in the hospital for a few days. For those who haven't experienced that, I'll try to paint you a picture. A typical day for me in the hospital: vitals and lab work at six thirty in the morning, breakfast at seven, either a walk or a shower, meds at nine, TV or playroom till a quarter after eleven, walk around the floor, lunch at noon, TV till three, walk around the floor, TV till five, supper at five thirty, another walk, and either TV or visitors till eight thirty at night. Mom was allowed to stay till nine thirty, but then they kicked her out. I had meds again at nine at night, vitals for the last time at ten thirty, and would be in bed by eleven, when the night shift nurse would come in to check on me and introduce herself. By the way, because of all the TV I was watching, I had memorized the ABC family lineup of shows. Sometimes my days would be broken up with x-rays, rounds, visitors, mail, showers, breathing treatments, and various other things (like a walk outside the hospital in the freezing cold or down to glass solarium at Montefiore Hospital). Back at the apartment, I had friends (till they left), a pool, a weight room (not that I went here too much), hallways to walk, and my own bed to watch TV. If I got sick of TV, I simply pulled out my laptop and popped in a DVD.

At the apartment, I also got mail, visitors, and outings if I was feeling good. My mom was good about outings. Sometimes she said we were going for a walk outside. Here's the thing: I'm a country girl, not a city girl. I hated all the traffic, noise, sirens, people, and so on. When I would feel well enough, we'd go shopping, out to the movies, for a long walk around the city, that kind of thing. My cousin and her then boyfriend/fiancé would come to see me at either the hospital or the apartment. One time she came to take me shopping so Mom could have a break. She took me to a big shopping mall, and she was a personal trainer, so she wouldn't allow me to get a wheelchair. She helped me to walk the entire loop of the mall. It hurt, but she told me she was proud of me when we were done. My friend Matt came out several times to see all of us who had transplants, and he went with my family to the mall at least once. I wasn't well enough that time to walk the mall, so we got a wheelchair, and he pushed me through the mall. He was so patient with me even when I was crabby and awful to him, and I thank God for his friendship even today. Another person who was patient with me even when I said awful things to her was Lidia. She would just sit there and take it. I asked her why she didn't just leave me behind. Her answer stunned me, and even now, I thank God for her words of wisdom.

She told me, "Nothing that you say or do to me will make me love you any less. I have loved you like a daughter and I will always love you like a daughter."

I have since apologized to her for the way I acted, but her words are forever burned in my memory. At one point, around the time of my rejection, Mom and I were sitting outside at the cathedral bench next to the hospital. I remember it clearly because the air wasn't so cold, but it smelled clean.

I looked up at Mom and said,   "I need to go home. Spring is coming without me."

I'm the kind of person who likes to be outside in the sunshine, fresh air, and cool breeze. Being told by the doctor that we could go home was incredible. Mom and I were sure I would only get a weekend pass (to go home Thursday and return Monday).

Dr. Sindhi said, "How far away do you live?"

We told him only four hours away, and we had a local ER if we needed it. He surprised us by saying we can go home for two whole weeks! I was so excited to be going home! Dad had been coming out every weekend and Audrey every other weekend. I got so many presents and cards from people that we sent Dad home with a full carload each weekend. When Dr. Sindhi said I could leave, we packed up the Escape and headed home. I had so much stuff that Dad couldn't even see out the back windows, and I couldn't lie down to nap! I had gotten a sleep shirt that read "Home Sweet Home" with Taz from my aunt and cousin and was under strict orders not to wear it till I could go home. That was where I was headed—home sweet home! Dad blew his horn as we left Pittsburgh, and I'm sure the other drivers were wondering if he was blowing at them.

When we got home, I went up to my room. If I remember correctly, the first thing I did going up the stairs was trip and land on my stomach. (I was still recovering.) In my room, I got quite a shock! Dad and Audrey had been putting my gifts and things in my room, and now I couldn't even walk through it! My cat didn't know me anymore, so I had to take five kitty treats to get her to come to me again, but it was worth it. Sleeping at home was amazing, and Mom was right about something. My attitude began to do a 180 for the better because I was surrounded by familiar things. On my first Sunday home, I went to church with my parents (I wasn't allowed to drive a car yet). Everybody was so excited to see me yet so afraid to make me sick. I had written a thank-you letter to the church, which my pastor read aloud during the sharing service. I didn't mean to make him choke up, but he was moved by what I had said.

A few days after I'd come home, Mom took me up to my work to say hi. I remember walking into the office, and everyone at the front desk went nuts. I had been in constant contact with my boss, and she let everyone else know what was going on.

The office manager and the CEO were working the front desk that day, and my boss said, "Can you come back today?"

She was only half kidding because four of the front desk girls called out sick that day. As I was leaving the office, a patient I had gotten to know fairly well was there for an appointment, and she stopped me for a hug. I didn't mind, but I also didn't want to get sick. She told me it was a checkup from a cold a while back, so I was okay. It was tough for me to sit around doing nothing since I'm the kind of person who thrives on a routine, always on the go. Since I had the rejection and was on a ton of meds, my appetite would come and go. On the steroids (prednisone and celcept), my appetite was crazy big. Even though I had lost weight, I don't recommend the diet plan. The upside about losing the weight was that I no longer looked heavy. In fact, I could wear my sister's outgrown jeans! Because I was in the hospital over Audrey's birthday, Mom said we could celebrate it late. She chose Ichaban's Japanese Grill. I was sure I wouldn't like anything there, and because of transplant, I had to be careful about what I ate. It was more entertaining to watch the chef than it was to actually eat it. I still wasn't totally well, so food didn't really taste good yet.

I had to laugh as we watched our chef tossing huge knives in the air, lighting big fireballs, and chopping food like it was disappearing before him! I remember wondering how he knew when the food was done because it was in flames. I liked the flaming onion train, and for those of you who have never been to a restaurant like this, it's crazy! The chef gets and onion and slices it down in rings, carefully arranging it in a tower form. He pours liquids (not sure if it's cooking oil or what) on it, and with flair, he lights it with a whoosh! As its cooking, he pushes it across the grill toward the other vegetables while making a lot of train noises (whoo whoo, chugga chugga, whoo whoo). It's pretty cool to see if you've never seen it before. Anyway, I didn't eat much that night, but I shared with Dad.

When our two weeks were up, we headed back to Pittsburgh for a clinic visit. The doctors came in after I had labs drawn and said everything looked good. We were allowed to return home.

Chapter 7

Another Stay at Pittsburgh

The day after we got home, Mom and I were coming home from shopping when I got a call on my cell phone from Pittsburgh. They told me that the one test they did came back positive for CMV, cytomegalovirus, a virus that most everyone has been exposed to but I had not been. The virus showed up because my donor had been exposed and I had not, thus causing cross contamination and flaring up due to heavy immunosuppression. They said I had to come back to Pittsburgh to get testing and medications. I begged them to let me just go to Lancaster General Hospital instead of out there, but they refused. When I got off the phone, I told Mom what they said and promptly burst into tears. How could I face being stuck in the hospital again? I was just getting my freedom back!

We left for Pittsburgh at two thirty in the morning because none of us could sleep anymore. I couldn't sleep because I was upset about being put in the hospital again, and my parents couldn't sleep because they were upset too. The drive was long and silent, as we were all lost in our own thoughts. When we got there, the room wasn't even ready yet. They said to be at the hospital by nine in the morning so we could start treatment. It turned out I didn't get my first treatment till that night. I remember being so bored because I felt okay but was hooked up to an IV machine again. This time I had thought to bring a macramé project that I was working on—a large scarf.

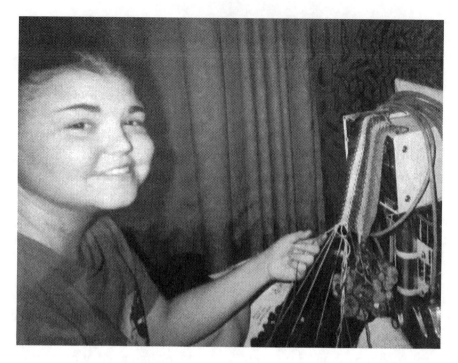

I figured if I was going to be stuck in the hospital again, I might as well have something constructive to do. I would hook up that scarf to the IV pole, turn on the TV, and get to work. I did finish it after my stay, which lasted a week and a half. My grandpa couldn't bear to have my mother out in Pittsburgh all alone, so he would send Grandma on the train out to see us. He came to see me only once, and I asked Mom why he wouldn't come again. She told me that he couldn't stand to see me hooked up to all the monitors and IVs like that.

The doctors told me that we had to do a PICC line this time because the medicine needed to fight the infection was too strong for a simple IV. I told the nurse that I wasn't taking no for an answer this time—that they were going to put me under and that was it.

I told her what had happened the last time and how the doctor said that wasn't how it was done, and she looked at me funny and said, "It's never done any other way. Your vein will constrict if you aren't sedated. You should have been sedated."

I told her I wasn't and asked whether she could please see that I was. She said of course she would. They were finally able to get a PICC line in, and thus began the twice-daily IV medication.

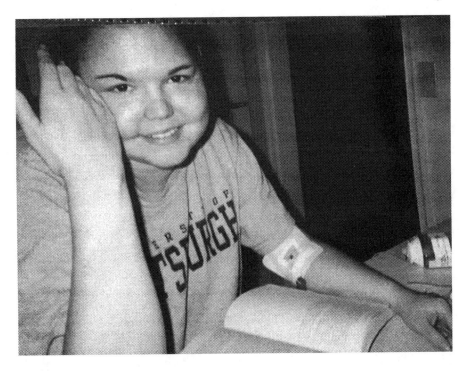

They discovered through another chest x-ray that I was still having some fluid buildup, so they put me on a water pill that did nothing for me. My mom and I stayed at a Ronald McDonald house farther from the hospital than last time but on the third floor! It had no elevator and no pool and was just really hard for me. It was hard going up and down the steps, as they were almost vertical. I loved the hallway window seat, though, which was nice and warm in the sunlight.

I had a nurse from visiting nurses come to change the bandages of the PICC line. When I was in the hospital for the final time, a reporter had gotten my name from the coordinator and interviewed me for the paper. Yes, I was in the Pittsburgh paper with a picture of me and my lucky (Care Bear) bear.

My cousin and her fiancé came to see me at the house, and he said, "I want to shake the hand of the local celebrity."

I'll never forget that. I never thought of myself as a celebrity, but when I see how many articles were done on me from both the transplant and MSUD, I guess I kind of am a celebrity. Since I was out in Pittsburgh over Easter, Mom and I celebrated Easter with my aunt and uncle who live there, plus my three cousins, one fiancé, and my mom's sister, who came to see her daughter that weekend. I was glad to get away from the house for a while, and it was a great time with my family. When we got back to the house, an accident happened in the front yard. I remember being up our room, relaxing and thinking that the sirens weren't getting quieter. When I told Mom, she remembered hearing a thump, and then we heard the sirens. We went downstairs, only to realize the sirens were in the front yard of the house.

A minivan from Pennsylvania had tried to make a left-hand turn onto the street below at the same time a little car from Ohio was trying to make a left-hand turn to go up past the house. I'm not too sure what happened exactly, but I remember seeing the van with the front end smashed in and the doors all open. The car was resting against the dogwood tree in the front yard with a deep rut in the grass behind it. If I remember correctly from the article, four people were taken to the hospital (and I think there were seven people altogether) despite the fact that the cops had to use the Jaws of Life to open the car up. No one was killed, and I think they were all treated and released. I remember the woman who owned the house was really angry that her yard was torn up and her tree smashed into by a car. She didn't care about the people, only her precious yard. I was just glad later that no one died, because from the looks of the accident, it could have been a lot worse.

When we were finally able to go home for good, I still needed to have a nurse come to change the bandages from my PICC line. The condition I had made it impossible not to have a PICC line, as I needed to take IV meds twice a day. I started kind of getting back to my life but not fully. I couldn't work just yet, so I had to stay home and rest, which was boring for me. When I had my checkups out in Pittsburgh, I asked when I would be allowed to go back to work. They couldn't give me an exact date, but I had to be as good as possible. Mom was good about taking me to restaurants so I could learn how to eat normal foods. I didn't like about 85 percent of the new foods I tried, simply because I didn't grow up eating that way.

My friends who had transplants with me didn't have problems eating food the way I did. They got used to new stuff in a hurry. Bri didn't have problems eating, but it turns out she was allergic to the one food she really liked—shellfish. I can't stand seafood (at least not much of it), so this I just couldn't understand. E is Jewish and shouldn't have been eating red meats, but because he wasn't allowed to eat it before, his priest made an exception. E spent a month in the hospital in May 2006 with a super-stubborn bout of rejection, requiring several different steroids and more meds than I could count. He did get over it, and we are all doing well as of late.

At home, things were getting better, with my labs still showing that I was doing as well as could be expected. I was adjusting to eating, though it was taking a long time, but I was trying very hard. In May 2006, our church suffered the loss of our active pastor. He died very suddenly from a massive heart attack, leaving a wife and two young boys. It was incredibly hard on everyone to get over that loss. One thing that made it sort of easier was that he was an organ donor. Lidia, his wife and the one who stayed with me, honored his wish and donated his organs. I asked her a few months later if she ever wanted to meet any of the people who had received his organs, and her answer surprised me.

"I'd rather not meet them. I want to remember him as he was before he died."

This kind of gave me insight to my donor's family. They never answered any of my letters, and I couldn't understand why they wouldn't at least acknowledge the letters. I found out more about my donor later on, but I can see now why they wouldn't want to see me.

When I was finally able to return to work five and a half months after the transplant, it took time to adjust to life again. I was tired more easily for a while because of the anesthesia used during the transplant. When I was able to go home, Dad had a surprise for me; he had had my car (a white 2004 Nissan Sentra) completely detailed inside and out. It never sparkled so well before!

Chapter 8

Mismatched Memories of Pittsburgh from My Pictures

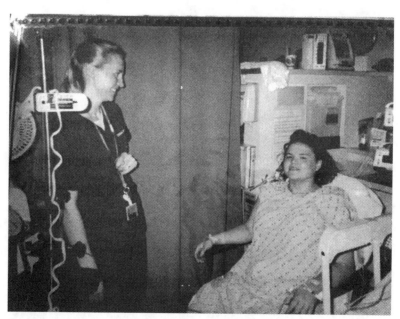

In the ICU, I had to learn how to get out of bed to prove I was ready for my next room. A physical therapist helped me get out of bed because I wasn't strong enough to do it on my own.

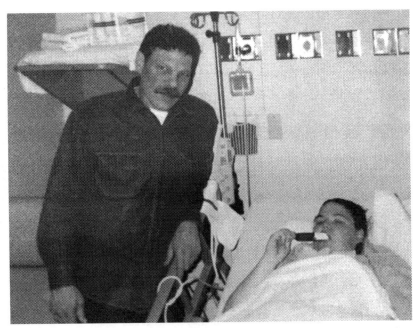

My first day up to the new room on 7N, my dad's brother got me a Reese's peanut butter ice cream bar. I took about five bites of it and decided it was too sweet for my liking.

Someone donated Terrible Towels to 7N for all the kids there. The playroom nurse gave me one, but she didn't know that I already had two! I actually had one of my towels signed by Dan Kreider, number 35 for the Steelers then.

Bri was going back home, so her mom brought her to say good-bye to me. I remember being jealous because I was still in the hospital and she was going back home for good.

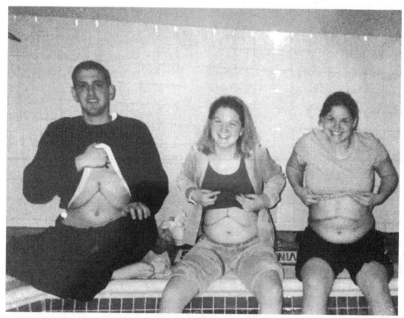

This picture is of the three of us at the pool showing off our new scars. As you can see, there is a variety in the sizes and even the placement of the scars.

In the hospital during my rejection stay, the amount of steroids made me very hungry. For the first time in my life, I could order whatever I wanted and didn't have to wonder if it would make me sick!

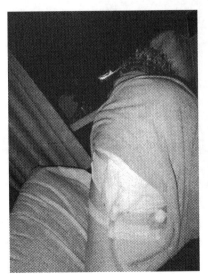

These pictures show the chest tube in my back to draw out the fluid and also just how bad I felt with it in my chest.

This was taken in the education room in the Cathedral of Learning, an active part of the University of Pittsburgh. There are eight rooms that depict different cultures, and we visited them with my cousins.

In order to come to see me (either in PICU or 7N), Mom and Dad and any visitors had to sign in. The lines for sign in showed some different people. Once there was even a Plain family that came to see someone.

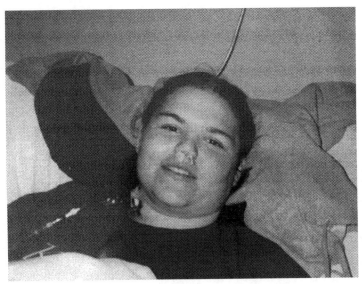

One time, after taking the awful nystatin, I had a piece of gum pressed to my nose hoping the smell would cover the taste. I got tired of holding it, and I wasn't allowed to chew it, so I broke it in half and stuck the pieces in my nose. It worked. The smell covered the taste, but Mom called me a rhino because she said it looked like I had tusks coming out of my nose!

When I was allowed to wear my own clothes, most of the outfits had Steelers in or on it in some form. However, there was a shirt I loved that Mom made me leave there that read, "Kiss Me, I'm American."

When I felt well enough, the transplant director said that E and I could walk down to the pathology lab with her to see our livers they had removed from us. That is something that I'm betting *no one else* can say they've done before—unless, of course, you've had a transplant!

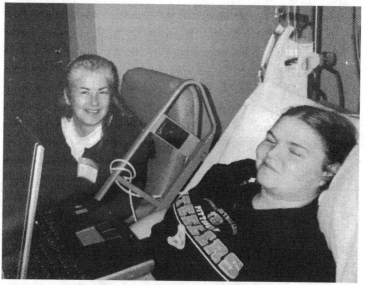

I had brought my laptop to the hospital and tried to play my Sims game on it during the rejection stay, but more than once, I found it extremely difficult to focus on the screen. Since everything seemed to jump across the screen, I eventually decided it wasn't worth the hassle.

Once when Grandma was staying at the apartment with us, Mom and I convinced the van driver to drive us down to the Shadyside Mall even though she wasn't supposed to go that far. We had to walk all around the mall, which was outdoors, and I wasn't feeling good at all. We found the movie theater where *Curious George* was playing, and I was happy to be able to sit down for a while. Grandma and I had gotten snacks at the concession stand, and we were sitting for the movie. The whole time we were waiting for the movie to start, Grandma kept saying, "I can't believe I'm sitting here watching a picture!" She had never gone to the movies before. Afterward we called Grandpa and told him we went to a movie. He said, shocked, "You got your grandma to watch a picture!"

During my final hospital stay, Grandma was sitting with me over lunch. She ate what I couldn't finish of my hotdog, then promptly sat back in her chair, head tipped back a little, and fell asleep. My transplant coordinator stopped by to see how I was doing and saw her in the chair. She looked at me and asked, "What did you do to her?" I said, like a smart aleck, "I fed her!" She got a good laugh out of that.

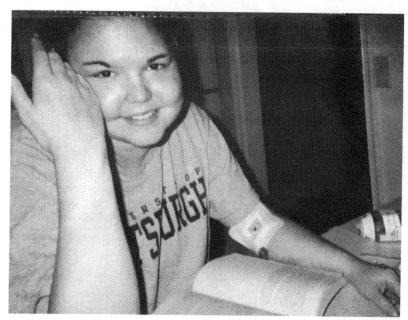

With the IV medicine, I had to learn how to give myself the medicine as well as flush the line before and after the medicine with saline. It was kind of fun and kind of a pain. It usually took about forty-five minutes to get everything done.

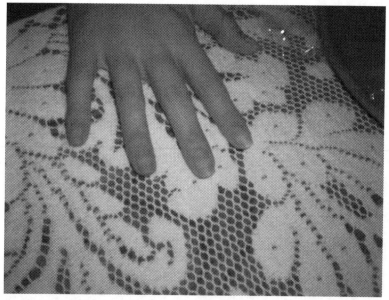

After my transplant, within the first few months, my nails started to grow in thicker than before transplant, and for a while you could see a definite line between the two types of nails. It was a white dent in the nail bed, and it was quite cool to see.

At one year, my parents took my family out to Olive Garden to celebrate life. I loved being able to eat what I wanted, and if I remember correctly, I had salad, breadsticks, and the Tuscan garlic chicken. We also shared a bottle of sparkling grape juice instead of alcohol.

***

After that first year, things got better for me. Eating got easier, but I was still very leery about eating protein. Since I needed to get more protein than before, Mom and Dad tried so hard to get me to eat. At one point, my parents actually thought I was anorexic because I wanted to eat low-protein foods. It was hard for me to start eating what I knew to be poison to me. I remember my dad becoming upset with me because I wouldn't eat the cheese off my pizza. To me, it was too slimy, too different of a texture for me to enjoy. Mom had to get creative to get me to eat protein. A neighbor suggested that since I loved corn, she could mix corn with eggs, milk, whipping cream, and sugar and bake it. That really helped me!

Maybe it's not very healthy, but it was awesome! To this day, Mom's corn pudding is one of my favorite recipes and one of the easiest to make.

Other ways I got the necessary protein, since I didn't like milk then, was I would mix carnation instant breakfast powder (French vanilla) with orange juice. As I grew to like other foods, I would mix things together. I always had a strange way of eating. Since with MSUD everything tasted the same, I had to get creative to change the taste. I always thought that perhaps the reason the Heinz Ketchup company is still in good business is because of MSUD. Every MSUD child loves ketchup, and it makes everything taste so much better.

I think after it was all said and done, it took a full nine and a half months after the transplant to feel like myself. Working at the doctor's office was a bit of a challenge, but I love challenges. I felt like my donor's family had something against me because I got their loved one's liver, but after speaking with Lidia about her husband, I realized it wasn't me they couldn't see. I believe even after all this time, they are still having a bit of difficulty accepting the death of their loved one. Praise God they had the clarity of mind to give her organs to someone like me for a new lease on life!

One memory I have from the hospital is one nurse who had to give me the nystatin. She was very understanding about the difficulty of taking this awful medicine. She had other patients to look after, but she gave me the nystatin and then stayed with me for twenty minutes, talking to me about my cat to get my mind off of the disgusting taste. It made a good impression on me.

In the two weeks I was home, I got to go to my sister's track meet. Being so thin, I couldn't get warm. It was springtime and not terribly cold, but to me, it was freezing! I had to be bundled from head to toe against the cold. I loved to watch Audrey in track and field and also in volleyball. I was proud of my sister! I still am proud of her, but then, she was breaking records in track as a freshman, and in track and volleyball, she was what they called super froshed—a freshman on a varsity team.

***

This picture of me was taken on my twenty-second birthday. My parents took me to Applebee's, where I ordered ribs with fries, and they allowed me to get a virgin daiquiri, along with a chocolate cake for dessert! Yum!

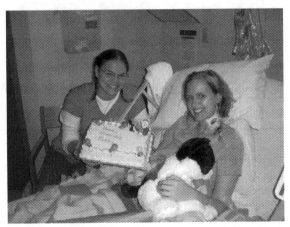

This is my best friend. She had her transplant one and a half years after I did. Here we are celebrating her birthday. We tried to surprise her, but she found out we were in town.

This picture was taken by my mother when we went to a local restaurant for lunch one day. I ordered honey-fried chicken and mashed potatoes with corn. Yum!

This pic was taken two years after my transplant, but these two went through it all with me! To my left is the main transplant coordinator, Lynn, and to my right is Dr. Mazareigos, the doctor who did my transplant.

This picture was taken before I returned to work. This is to show just how much weight I had lost. Those jeans are my sister's jeans! She was sooooo jealous!

This was my coordinator, Nicole. I had her for around three years. Dr. Sindyh was an awesome doctor!

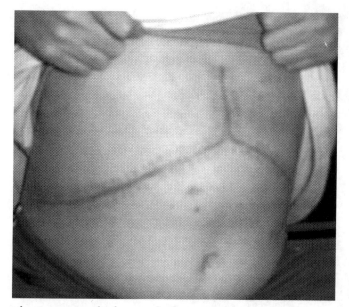 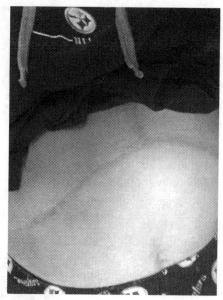

These two are before and after pics. The first one is from the first six months after transplant, and the second one is from now (almost ten years out of transplant).

Chapter 9

Mom and Dad's Journal Entries

My parents kept a sort of journal during the first six months after my transplant. Mom wrote more in the journal than Dad did, as it kept her from yelling at me.

9:00 p.m., Sunday, January 22—Kim called from Pitt. Said Amy will have a liver for her. Left the house at 9:25 p.m. Arrived in Pitt at 1:30 a.m. Went to the emergency department to register. Went to 7N, room 10. The nurses drew blood for amino acids. Sent to analyze STAT. Abby and Laura are our nurses. Her blood pressure was high, 139/93.

2:45 a.m.—The doctor came in room to have Amy sign for permission. He explained the procedure. They will give her a blood transfusion. Took a chest x-ray.

4:30 a.m.—Took (Amy) to the preop room; met Dr. Sindhi.

4:45 a.m.—She went into the OR, and we went over to the waiting room. We napped, called a few people, and prayed. At 6:30 a.m., Dr. Sindhi came in and said that things are going well. One artery was three-pronged, and so they will have to reconstruct (the main artery), so the surgery will take approximately forty-five minutes to one hour longer. Dr. Mazeregieos stopped in at about 10:15 to tell us that things were going well, that the new liver was in, but that they were still working on the artery. Dr. Sindhi also stopped in the waiting room a half hour later to let us know that Amy is doing well so far. We got sandwiches from the cafeteria.

12:15 p.m.—Nurse came in and said the liver was just about all sewn in, and then next they have to do the bowel duct.

Nine-hour surgery. Went to see her in ICU at 6:30 p.m. She had a breathing tube, and her eyes were closed. She was very pale. We took showers and went to bed early! Very, very tired! Exhausted! Went to see Amy first thing at 6:30 a.m. She was more alert!

She signed to us to communicate. Still has a breathing tube. Her throat was *very* dry. She had a fever overnight. She asked for her teddy bear! She asked when Matt was coming in to visit. We did not see E yet. Andra and Jacks sat with us for about two hours or so.

Tuesday, 2:30 p.m.—They took her breathing tube out. She looks *so* much better. More color in her face. They put Vaseline on her dry, chapped lips. She could suck on ice chips only. She was thirsty. Had to give her more blood. Her blood pressure was a little high.

Audrey—Livers can go up to eight hours on ice, but lungs and other organs are more sensitive and sometimes last only two hours.

Dad—Wednesday, January 24, 1:30 a.m.—Amy still had a very dry mouth. They gave her Prograf by breaking open the capsule and putting dry powder under her tongue. She begged for water but got none. At 6:00 a.m., the doctor was in again. Not much has changed, but her vital signs were good. At 8:00 a.m. the nurse said her vital signs were still good, but the blood drainage from stomach cavity was still too much, so they took her for an MRI to check about bleeding. Still no liquid by mouth, probably because of possibility of having to do more surgery.

Mom—10:30 a.m.—Not good news. She is going into surgery again to clean out a collection of blood that has formed behind the liver. Very upsetting! But we knew that it was a possibility. Surgery went well. I am getting a cold today. I wore mask to go in to see Amy.

Thursday—Amy got her NG tube out. The nurse cleaned her face up. She looks better now. Still very sleepy, but her mind is clear! Her blood pressure is still too high. They gave her something (diuretic) to make her pee. The pain she says is a four on a scale of one to ten. She's still on meds for pain. The hotel is very nice. Breakfast is included.

Dad—Friday, 12:15 p.m.—It's cold and clear today. We walked to the hospital. Amy had a restless night. She has a lot of pain and feels tight across her chest. Her blood pressure is high, and her heart rate is high. Her face is flushed, and she doesn't like her nurse. They gave her meds to bring her blood pressure down. The doctor said her symptoms are typical for her type of surgery. Her kidneys are working well, and her other vitals are pretty good. They said they are just trying to get her stabilized.

Mom—early Saturday morning—(They) moved Amy to intermediate ICU. She looks *so* much more like herself. Her blood pressure has come down now. She drank two quarts of water overnight. Wow!

Dad—Saturday, 4:30 p.m.—Amy was moved out of ICU and into her own room. She has a tough nurse, but she is good. She's not going to baby Amy. She stood up three times to walk to the bathroom because they took the catheter out of her. The nurse said that she could begin to have soft foods, but she's not hungry yet. They also stopped her IV drip because she's drinking enough.

Mom—Sunday morning—Went up to see Amy. She had gotten up to go to the bathroom several times. She is steadier on her feet now. She ate a little vanilla pudding. She asked for yogurt, but they didn't bring it up yet. We came back to the hotel to go to church with Amy's cousin and grandpa and grandma.

Monday—Amy had a bath today and got her hair done. She still has some pain. The drain was pulled even though a lot of drainage was still leaking out. She still has blood pressure problems. They gave her more medicine for blood pressure. Dad left to go home at 2:00 p.m. to be with Audrey and to light the stove at home. Audrey said the house was cold. He should be home by 6:00 p.m. or so.

Monday night—Amy is hooked up to an IV again. She is not getting enough food and fluids. She is eating very little. We are not pushing the matter. It is going to take a little time to get used to this new eating pattern. Her blood pressure is better.

Tuesday—She is walking up and down the hall feeling stronger. About 10:30 a.m. she vomited once. She was good the rest of the day and walked some more. Her blood pressure is good now 117/232. E went home today to the hotel.

January 31—She walked around more, less pain. She had to be given two units of blood for low blood count and dehydration. She's still on blood pressure medication and has no desire to eat. She had very little food today. My sister was here. She gave Amy a back rub and a foot massage. That made Amy really happy. We called a cousin and her mother tonight and talked on the phone for a while.

Amy was very tired today! She threw up after sucking on lozenge. She ate a very little more than yesterday. We went to the playroom and made Steelers banners. We walked to the library. Bri came in to await a transplant.

Friday—We viewed Amy's old liver today. Dad came back here at 10:00 p.m. Audrey had to stay home and work.

Saturday—Amy's aunt and uncle, along with two of their daughters, came to visit from 11:30 till 4:00 p.m. Amy walks more but doesn't eat very much. She's lost twelve pound already.

Sunday, February 5—Amy ate Salisbury steak, mashed potatoes, and gravy. She said, "It's not bad!" She walked more today. She still gets tired but feels a lot better.

Tuesday—Discharged to the hotel with fifty-eight staples in her stomach.

Tuesday evening, February 28 till Wednesday March 2—In hospital. Sick—nausea, fever.

March 3, Friday—She still has a fever. They decided to do liver biopsy to be sure she's not rejecting. Her liver numbers are good!

Sunday March 12—Beck and Jas got engaged.

March 13, Monday—It's a nice day, warm outside. We went outside to enjoy it. I looked into Amy's mouth and saw white spots! Told PA Tami as soon as we got back. If it's thrush, she will have to use nystatin four times a day. Her sugars are 130.

Amy looks pretty good—nice color, more excitement for life. She eats more food now. I brought stuff from home—pork chops and rice with peas. She was very happy to eat that! Grandma H sent some home-canned peaches and applesauce. Amy really enjoyed that!

Good Friday, April 14—This is awful. All we do is give medications, blood pressures, temps, and more pills, pills, and pills. I'm so sick of nurses and hospitals and pills! Amy doesn't even want to eat protein foods! Ronald McDonald house is nice. I like our room and the common kitchen and living room.

These journal entries gave me insight to my parents' struggle with what happened with me. As you can see, a transplant affects everyone in the family. While my sister didn't write in the journal, I suspect she had her own struggles. She was forced to grow up as much as I was during that time. She was a junior in high school, so she had to go to school, run the house, and work part-time. I think during the first six months, as happy as she was for me, she probably felt a bit neglected.

Chapter 10

Adjusting to Life after Transplant

Life after transplant took a long time to adjust. I went back to work full-time in June 2006 as a receptionist. It was hard, but over time, I learned how to adapt to my new normal. My thinking got clearer, my impulsiveness wasn't as bad, and communication wasn't so frustrating. Even eating got easier. Mom learned little tricks to get more protein into my system, which helped with the healing. By my twenty-second birthday, September 13, I was able to eat more protein, and the one food I loved to eat at that time was a barbequed hamburger done Mennonite style. It was amazing to smell growing up and even more amazing to eat! Paired just right with potato rolls and my favorite chips, it was an amazing high-protein meal that I could finally eat!

For my birthday, Dad took me to a local buffet restaurant where my meal was free (since it was my birthday), and I loaded up my plate with all the things I couldn't have before: real mashed potatoes, baked corn, roasted chicken, ham and green beans, and more, including desserts like cookies, Amish-made whoopee pies, and even real chocolate pudding. You can imagine that it was fun for me to be able to do this finally, but it was a struggle to wrap my brain around it. Dad did tell me that he was so proud of me for eating my chicken! That was so wonderful to hear after their frustration with me and eating.

I will include a chapter of recipes that helped me to adjust to eating that include my tweaks on them. I have to tweak stuff because some things are harder to eat than others. By the time the first anniversary of my transplant rolled around, we had gone out to Pittsburgh a month early for my cousin's wedding and for my checkup. My family decided to go to Olive Garden for the celebration. I ordered a dish that sounded great to me, but the best thing was being able to finally eat those awesome breadsticks! We brought a bottle of sparkling grape juice for our meal, and the waitress was okay with that once she knew why I couldn't have alcohol.

Two years after my transplant, while working full-time at Welsh Mountain, I went to a wedding in September 2008 of a friend. While there, I remet a close friend I hadn't seen for four years since the bride (who is his cousin) had her graduation party. In talking with him, I realized that I wanted to get to know him again, so I gave him my number and said I wanted to get together for coffee or ice cream or something to catch up on our lives.

That started the romance of my husband and me, all because I pursued him instead of the other way around. Randy was the best thing that happened to me, especially when it came to food. Our first date was on my twenty-third birthday. He told me to dress nicely because he was taking me for Thai food. I had had Chinese food before and loved it, so I thought Thai couldn't be that much different. At first it was a little awkward. We had changed so much in four years that the first things we talked about was our time together at our church years before. When we first moved there, he was my best church friend. We did everything together because I was a tomboy—no makeup, dresses, or high heels for this little girl! With jeans, a T-shirt, sneakers, and my hair in a ponytail ... I'm good. Another reason Randy and I got along so well was we were both different. He is a two-time leukemia survivor (ALL), and I had MSUD. His eyes were lazy too. When he looked at me back then, his left eye looked at me mostly and his right drifted past me. I used to ask him if he was sure he could see me clearly. He always said he could, but I never knew if he really could see me.

On that first date, we talked about the things we used to do at church together and laughed about the skit we were in for Christmas. That skit was so funny for us! I was on the voice and stage crew, and his job was to move the car as if it was driving and then pull the board when it "crashed." It still makes me laugh. Randy encouraged me to try the chicken and jasmine rice on our date, which turned out to be wonderful. In the course of talking, we found out that we both had a love of mini golf. He suggested that we go and play a round after dinner. However, we weren't counting on the change of weather. When we went into the restaurant, it was cloudy but not raining. After our meal, we came out to a thunderstorm. That cancelled mini golf, but then he told me that his parents had an awesome big screen and we could rent movies. We did just that, and he ended up bringing me home around one o'clock in the morning. What a great first date!

That began an inseparable relationship between us. We had so many dates and just hang nights where we talked about everything. By the time we started talking about getting married, my family was wondering if he was ever going to pop the question. I had my own apartment by that time and was still working at the doctor's office. Randy and I spent a lot of time at each other's homes during the year and a half of dating. By August

2009, he was thinking of proposing. He had a plan to propose to me on Saturday, but he wanted to use a sign to ask me to marry him. This plan meant that he had to duck me for an entire week while he and another friend painted this sign together. He went to the local car wash and detailer to get his truck cleaned inside and out. He told the guys there that he was going to propose to his girlfriend, so they made sure to make it sparkle. Carrying the sign to my parents' house and coordinating everything with my family without me knowing about it wasn't easy. They kept his secret, and he avoided me like crazy that week. By the time the end of the week rolled around, I was thoroughly angry with him.

However, when I got to my parents' house and saw him with that sign, I forgot about being mad at him. I rolled up the driveway with my little blue car, and as I got out of the car, I looked at him and said, "You know my answer to this."

I never told him yes, but he knew because I wanted nothing more than to marry him. His parents, my parents, and my sister were witnesses to the moment of his proposal, and I will never forget how shaky we both were after it was all over. The next few weeks were spent telling people the story of our engagement and even how we met as we began to plan our future.

In October, I took my hardest-to-fit bridesmaid (my best friend) to find a dress that would fit her frame at a dress store I never knew was there. As we found her dress as well as the other bridesmaids' dresses, I also found my dress. I had been looking at every style and design possible and couldn't quite find one to my liking. This dress fit like it was made just for me. It didn't have too much bling on it, but it wasn't too plain either. The train wasn't so long that I would rip it off if I stepped on it by accident, but it wasn't so short that it looked ridiculous on my five-foot, four-inch frame. By doing research, I found out that wedding dresses are made for brides that stand at five feet, nine inches or taller, and then a seamstress makes a lot of money by charging an arm and a leg in alterations. The lady I used to do my alterations luckily didn't have to do a ton of alterations for me. She did a bustle and pulled the dress straight up under the rouching at my stomach.

The day of my wedding to Randy was gorgeous!

The sun was shining, it was warm, and our colors looked awesome! My mom had some concerns that teal green and lavender didn't go together well till she saw the colors together. Now she says that we had the best color combo she's ever seen at a wedding! I treated my girls to an earring and necklace set to wear at the wedding and even paid for the hairdos at a local salon.

Audrey and I had our nails done together, and I must say, it was a blast! She was excited that she was gaining a brother at last. When we first got engaged, I think she was worried about it, but as time went on and she got to know him, she began to really like him. At my wedding, Audrey was my maid of honor, so she had to make a speech. I must admit, I had no idea what she was going to do or say. At my bridal shower, she had everyone help her with a Mad Libs that she wrote for me because she knew I loved Mad Libs. In her speech, she told our getting-together story.

Looking at Randy, she said, "I know Randy doesn't like when I tell this story, but I'm gonna tell it anyway. Amy and Randy met at his cousin's wedding—or I guess I should say remet, as they knew each other as kids. If you knew Amy in her earlier years, no guy ever intimidated her at all. She was the pursuer in a relationship. She saw something she wanted, and she would go after it. She had asked Randy if she ever stood a chance with him, and he answered with an epic, 'No thank you, you're not my type.' Amy kind of shrugged it off, but in 2008, she saw Randy again at his cousin's wedding. This time she wanted to see him again, so she asked for his number and kind of hinted that her birthday was coming up. He took the hint to ask her out on a date, and he took her for Thai food. This is why I believe Randy is good for my sister, because before he came along, Amy was really picky about trying any kind of new foods. Randy, this is how you bring out the best in my sister. And I can't see her with anyone else."

It was a beautiful speech but not quite accurate. While I did ask Randy if I stood a chance with him and that was his answer, he wasn't the one who asked me out after the wedding. I told him I wanted his number so we could get together for coffee or ice cream or something to catch up on our lives since it had been four years since I had seen him last. He was the one who suggested dinner instead. I had never tried Thai food before, and with MSUD, I wouldn't have even been able to have it. I've tried all kinds of foods, thanks to Randy.

Chapter 11

Life as It Is Now

Today I am a happily married wife of a truck driver. Both of us are employed full-time, and my "child" is a four-legged fur baby (cat) named Trixie. I would love to sit here and tell you that life has been one breeze after another since transplant, but that would be a bald-faced lie. After the transplant, you learned about my immediate complications, but since I've been married, there have been more complications. Six months after we said "I do," I learned that I had miscarried our first and only child.

My dreams of that baby I was carrying, or should I say nightmare, indicated I was carrying a little boy. Randy and I had chosen to name him Caleb Joel even though he resides in heaven, along with my grandfather, Randy's grandmother, and my cousin who died in 2004. I don't wish to indulge in my nightmare, as it still gives me creeps even though it's been five years since it happened. I will say this about that nightmare ... I woke up from a sound sleep bawling. Randy had already left for work, so I called him or texted him (I don't remember which I had done) and told him of the dream. Needless to say, I didn't sleep for the rest of the night. A few weeks later, we learned of the missed miscarriage at a routine office visit. A missed miscarriage is when the fetus dies, but the body does not expel the dead fetus. In most cases, the woman's symptoms of pregnancy (tenderness, morning sickness, etc.) usually disappear when the baby dies, but in my case, I still had all the symptoms of pregnancy. It turns out that my body was still trying to pump blood to a dead fetus. I found out at an office visit with the high-risk ob-gyn. I had to see a high-risk doctor due to the transplant, taking multiple medications, and a host of complications.

I knew when the nurse was doing the ultrasound that something was wrong. She wouldn't look at me, answer any of my questions, or even leave the monitor on. When the doctor came in, he did two ultrasounds, and then he had me sit up. He told me in a quiet voice that he was sorry, but the baby was gone. He said that judging by the length of the baby, he was nine weeks along, and I would have been eleven weeks at that point. I took it okay for a few minutes, and then it hit me—my baby was dead! Thank God Randy was able to be with me at that appointment. I could tell he was trying to be strong for me, but he was devastated too. I was supposed to have come back from vacation that night to work the evening shift.

I called my supervisor and told her that I wasn't coming in since I'd just found out I had lost my baby. All my coworkers knew I was pregnant, and they all knew how much I wanted to be a mother. I was told later that when the supervisor got off the phone with me, she told the other receptionists (she had told me not to worry about that evening; someone else would work for me), and all the receptionists started crying when they found out. They knew how excited I was about being a mom. We went to each set of parents' homes to let them know of the miscarriage. The first set of parents we visited was Randy's mom and dad. They had my sister-in-law's hyperactive labradoodle, who normally greets everyone with crazy jumping and barking.

That night when we came in the door, she bolted around the corner in her usual spastic way but stopped short, as if she hit an invisible wall. She put her head down and padded quietly to my side. I walked into the living room sadly, and she followed me, only steps behind. When I sat down on the couch, she sat at my feet and put her head sadly on my knees. She knew I needed quiet and a friend. She didn't move from my side till we left. The hardest part was telling both sets of parents they weren't going to be grandparents anymore. It took two procedures to get everything out of my uterus, and then I was given the news that because of that miscarriage, I can no longer have my own children. I had to have a tubal ligation for medical reasons (not that I agreed with any of them) and have had to resign myself to the fact that I will only be Aunt Amy instead of Mommy.

Since that miscarriage, Randy and I have had some bumps along the way, but for us, divorce will never be an option. We have resolved to work out our issues in Christian counseling, and I believe the miscarriage has made us stronger as a couple. My sister-in-law had my beautiful niece in March 2015, and my own sister had my adorable nephew in November of 2015. I am so lucky to be their aunt!

We've made some awesome memories as husband and wife and with our families. One year for Christmas, his dad gave all of us kids a sailing weekend in northeast Maryland. Another year, he gave us a Caribbean cruise. We've gone to the beach with my family, and we've had awesome Christmas get-togethers. A Christmas gift from Randy to me was two tickets to see our favorite group, Rascal Flatts, in concert at Hershey's Giant Center.

Anniversary trips to the beach and to different states have proven to be wonderfully relaxing. Things like our sanity trips (one or two nights in a hotel outside of Lancaster County) help to keep us fresh together.

If I can make anything stick from this book, it's that organ donation is a wonderful gift to someone like me, an unselfish act that can give another person a second chance. Despite what people say, the doctors will not let you die just because you're an organ donor. What happens is if you are beyond any kind of medical help (a stroke or heart attack that killed you), but your organs are still healthy, then the organ donation team (Gift of Life or Angel Flight or a similar organization) will approach your family and encourage them to donate your organs. Just because your driver's license says you are a donor doesn't mean they will harvest you as soon as they can. It just means you want someone else to get a second chance at life, but you must make your family aware of your choice. They are the ones who decide what happens to your organs after your death. Please sign up to give someone like me a second chance.

I will be honest—I've struggled with depression and even wanted to die after I lost my baby, but I realized that since I'm an organ recipient, it would be a waste to throw away my life after my donor's family went through such heartache to make the decision to give their loved one's organs away. One person can donate heart, lungs, kidneys, liver, pancreas, stomach, large and small intestines, bone marrow, body tissue, corneas, and even skin. That's a lot of lives that can be saved. Please consider becoming a donor. It only takes a few minutes to register.

Chapter 12

My Favorite Recipes

Corn pudding is one of the recipes my mother used after my transplant to help me learn to eat protein. I was allowed to have corn and I couldn't taste the milk or eggs, so this recipe quickly became my favorite.

Corn Pudding
 1/4 cup of sugar
 3 tablespoons flour
 2 teaspoons baking powder
 1 1/2 teaspoons salt
 6 large eggs
 2 cups heavy whipping cream
 1/2 cup melted butter
 6 cups fresh corn (12 ears)

Mix ingredients in a large bowl and pour into a 9-by-13 pan. Bake at 350 degrees for 45 minutes, covered with foil.

Pork chops and rice was a recipe my mom would make for our family. As a kid, I couldn't have the pork chops, but I was allowed to have the rice and soup mix. Love this recipe even more now that I can have the pork chops.

Pork Chops and Apples with Rice

 4 pork chops, thin cut
 1 tablespoon vegetable or peanut oil
 1/2 cup apple juice
 1 package of Knorr Vegetable Soup Mix (yellow pack)
 2 red apples, sliced
 1 onion, chopped

Brown chops on both sides in oil. Add apple juice and soup mix; simmer 20 minutes. Add apples and onion. Cover and simmer 10 minutes more. Serve over rice.

Barbecue baked beans go really well with hot dogs or hamburgers and are the perfect side dish for a cookout. This recipe I alter a little bit, as I don't really measure the ketchup.

Barbecue Baked Beans

 2 (1-pound, 13-ounce) cans of baked beans (I use Bush's beans)
 1 pound bacon, fried and crumbled
 2 medium onions, finely chopped
 3 teaspoons Worcestershire sauce
 1 cup ketchup or don't measure
 1 cup brown sugar

Mix all ingredients together, and pour into a covered casserole dish. Bake at 325 degrees for 2 1/2 hours to 3 hours. Serves twenty people.

Chicken 'n' rice casserole is a staple with my family. Again, growing up, I was not allowed the meat of the chicken, but if my levels were good, I could have some skin of the chicken. I've tweaked this recipe a little by replacing celery soup with chicken soup. Delicious!

Chicken 'n' Rice Casserole

 1 cup rice, uncooked
 1 can cream of mushroom soup
 1 1/2 cups water

1 can cream of chicken soup
1 teaspoon salt
dash of pepper
4–6 chicken legs
optional—1/4 teaspoon of Cajun seasoning

Lay chicken pieces on top of the rice and soup mix. Bake at 375 degrees covered with foil for 2 hours.

Chickenetti is a recipe from my mother-in-law. It took me several times of making it to really enjoy it. This is my husband's favorite recipe.

Chickenetti

1 pound spaghetti noodles, cooked
4 cups cooked chicken, cut into bite size
2 cans cream of mushroom soup
1 can cream of celery soup
1 1/2 cups milk
2 cups chicken broth
1/4 teaspoon pepper
1/4 teaspoon celery salt
1 pound cheese, cubed or grated (Velveeta cheese preferred)
Sprinkle with bread crumbs.

Mix together. Bake at 350 degrees for 1 hour covered and then 10 minutes uncovered.

Baked oatmeal is an amazing breakfast or anytime casserole and so easy to make! I like to use apple filling in my baked oatmeal.

Baked Oatmeal

1/2 cup oil
2 eggs
for a sweet taste, add 1 can of your favorite pie filling on the bottom of the pans
2 teaspoons baking powder
1 cup milk
1 cup sugar

    3 cups oatmeal
    1 teaspoon salt

Mix together oil, sugar, and eggs. Add baking powder, milk, salt, and oatmeal. Pour into a greased cake pan, and bake at 350 degrees for 30 minutes. Serve hot with milk.

Zippy glazed carrots is a recipe that I could have even before transplant. My mom would make this for every holiday with her family so that I could at least eat something. The glaze part always is good to mix into mashed potatoes.

Zippy Glazed Carrots
    2 tablespoons margarine
    1/4 cup brown sugar
    2 tablespoons mustard (honey)
    1/4 teaspoon salt
    1 tablespoon parsley flakes
    3–4 cups cooked carrots

Mix together. Cook whole baby carrots or sliced regular carrots. Drain water. Add glaze and serve.

Mexican rice has always been my favorite recipe. Of course, on a bad day, I would have to halve the rice and keep everything else the same. My twist on this longtime favorite is to add 1/4 pound of browned ground beef in with the rice.

Mexican Rice
    1/2 cup uncooked white/brown rice
    1/2 clove garlic, minced
    1/2 cup tomatoes
    1 package Washington's broth
    1/4 cup chopped onion
    1 tablespoon vegetable/peanut oil
    1/2 teaspoon chili powder
    1 cup water

In a skillet, sauté rice, onion, and garlic in oil for several minutes or until rice is crackly and lightly golden. Stir in the remaining ingredients. Bring to a simmer; cover and cook over low heat for 20–30 minutes or until rice is tender. Fluff with a fork before serving. Yields 2 cups.

Lemon squares is an easy dessert; and if you love lemon like I do, you will love these squares!

Lemon Squares
    1 cup butter, softened
    1/2 cup confectioners' sugar
    2 cups flour
    1/4 teaspoon baking powder
    1/4 teaspoon salt

In a large bowl with an electric mixer at medium speed, beat butter and sugar until light and fluffy. In a small bowl, combine flour, baking powder, and salt. At low speed, gradually beat flour mixture into butter mixture until well blended. Press dough into 13-by-9-inch pan. Bake at 350 degrees for 20 minutes. Meanwhile, prepare the filling:

    4 large eggs
    2 cups sugar
    1/3 cup flour
    1/3 cup freshly squeezed lemon juice
    2 tablespoons grated lemon peel

In a large bowl, beat all ingredients for about 4 minutes until light and fluffy. Pour over baked crust; bake 30 minutes until set. When cool, sprinkle with confectioners' sugar. Cut into squares.

Easy company chicken is another one of those recipes that as a kid I loved but couldn't eat much of. This recipe never fails to please my husband or my father.

Easy Company Chicken
    up to 2 dozen chicken legs or thighs
    carrots
    potatoes cut up
    combine 1/2 cup ketchup
    1/4 cup water
    1/4 cup brown sugar

1 envelope of dry onion soup mix

Pour mix over chicken, potatoes, and carrots. Bake at 350 degrees for 1 1/2–2 hours.

***

That's my story, and I'm sticking with it! Ha-ha! I love that I can be so open and honest. Transplant is *not* by any means easy, and it's a lifelong commitment, but the alternative was living day to day not knowing when my disease would kill me. I wish more people would realize the value of life and the greatest act of giving your organs so someone else might have a chance. To the people already listed as donors, on behalf of all recipients, I thank you very much. The disease I was born with would have killed me in some way, but someone else died to save my life, just like Christ did for us. I am a Christian, and I'm not afraid to say it. I may step on people's toes and maybe it makes you uncomfortable, but I'm not letting it go. Christ died to save my life, and someone else died to give me another chance at life. Anyone can tell you that Jesus doesn't exist, but I want to know how you can believe that when you can see God in everything around you. For me, Jesus must want me here for some reason, because of all the things that could have taken my life, he allowed me to stay here. He brought me through the darkest of all my days, but it was not a cakewalk.

Life today for me is still rough. I'm dealing with residual effects from transplant that don't seem to go away, and I know several friends who also have a lot of complications. I will tell you this: I am thankful to my donor's family every day that they were willing to give their loved one's organs to people like me. I will end my story with a simple *thank you!*

Printed in the United States
By Bookmasters